A Review of the Book

UNITED STATES OF SOCIALISM

*Who's Behind It. Why It's Evil.
How to Stop It.*

by Dinesh D'Souza

Book Review by **WILLIAM E. SARACINO**
Executive Vice President, White House Watch Fund

Introduction by **SANT GUPTA**
(past) Master of Ceremonies, Freedom Leadership Conference

Review of **United States of Socialism** *by Dinesh D'Souza*, is published by FreedomPublishers.com for White House Watch Fund (formerly White House Defense Fund).

This is a Review, not the full 290-page book. Freedom Publishers is not associated with Dinesh D'Souza or the publisher of his book, which we recommend and which can be purchased at FreedomPublishers.com, Amazon.com or your local bookstore.

Book Review by William E. Saracino, Executive Vice President, White House Watch Fund

Introduction by Sant Gupta, (past) Master of Ceremonies, Freedom Leadership Conference

Special thanks to the following who have made the publishing of this review possible:

Associate Editor: Owen Jones

Executive Editor: Hanover Henry

Cover design and typesetting: Spencer Grahl

Amanda G. Hyland, Esq.
Taylor, English, Duma LLP, Atlanta, Georgia

This publication was made possible thanks to a grant from the Freedom Center Foundation.

This pocketbook and the organizations which have worked together to publish and circulate it do not advocate for or against candidates for local, state or federal office. Along with the author of *United States of Socialism*, we are fans of President Trump and strongly advocate for his agenda.

Copyright© July 2020, First Edition
Copyright© June 2021, Second Edition

Donations to pay for more copies of this pocketbook
to be printed and distributed may be made to:

White House Watch Fund
(formerly White House Defense Fund)
A project of United States Public Policy Council,
a 501(c)4 public policy corporation.
Donations not tax deductible.

WhiteHouseWatchFund.org

or mail

White House Watch Fund
Freedom Center, P.O. Box 820
Stuarts Draft, VA 24477-0820.

or

Freedom Center Foundation
Chairman@FreedomCenterFoundation.org

Gifts to the Foundation are tax deductible
on your federal tax return. Gifts of $1000 or
more are requested.
Recognized by IRS as a 501(c)3 charity.

Additional copies of this pocketbook may be ordered
for a gift of $5 each, 3 for $10, 10 for $20, 100 for
$150 plus postage and handling of $3 plus 10%.
Inquire for larger orders.

FreedomPublishers.com for online orders &
other books and pocketbooks including the hardcover
United States of Socialism book by Dinesh D'Souza.

INTRODUCTION

by Sant Gupta

Past Master of Ceremonies, Freedom Leadership Conference

Although I've been in America for 50 years, I am a first generation, new "American by Choice," not by accident of birth. So I do especially empathize with Dinesh D'Souza, one of my favorite filmmakers and authors, and a fellow American of Asian-Indian background and author of the new book, *United States of Socialism*.

Conservatives have to do a better job of explaining assimilation and its benefits to first generation, new Americans by Choice. We start off in this task with such an enormous advantage. After all, like me and Dinesh D'Souza, they made a choice to leave their country of origin and come to America. Why did we make that choice?

We must also do a better job of explaining America, to Americans, many of whom have been taken in by the false siren call of security and life-improvement offered by socialism.

The overwhelming answer most immigrants over the years always give, is they came to America for opportunity, the chance to raise their kids in freedom where they have the chance to improve themselves.

Just as the runaway slave Frederick Douglass freed himself, then was self-educated and ultimately assimilated and became a successful American who should be admired by all generations that came after him, all immigrants chose America because they have the chance to make something better of themselves.

Too many Americans who now embrace socialism forget that, to paraphrase Ronald Reagan, socialism is the equal sharing of misery and the tearing down of those more successful in the futile hope it will improve your life.

No wonder so many of society's "have-nots" —youth and blacks—have been tearing down monuments and statues showcasing America's heroes—including Lincoln and Douglass— and heritage.

Despite the fact that Socialism has been a failure in every country where it has been tried, it is more popular now today here in America, than ever. A 2019 Gallup survey reports that 43 percent of Americans—a record since World War II—say that Socialism would be a good thing for the United States.

The advocates of Socialism, whether they openly proclaim it with that name or simply proclaim its policies—are riding high and virtually control one political party and command the loyalty of an absolute majority of young people in the United States.

So I say, don't just worry about whether the new Americans by choice will join me and D'Souza as fully assimilated Americans. We'd better worry about introducing the greatness of America and how awful socialism is, to many Americans who appear more ignorant about it than many of the new arrivals.

I believe the new book, *United States of Socialism* by Dinesh D'Souza, is terrific. It is a needed book. It may even become a very consequential book that makes a major difference in whether America accepts and adopts or rejects socialism.

I am proud to enthusiastically support this cause by introducing to you, this review of his book, designed to help spread his ideas and hopefully, persuade many Americans to purchase the actual book. I hope you will consider this book review as the appetizer and go on to consume the "full course" and help make this a runaway bestseller. Thank you.

SOCIALISM. THE DISEASE KILLING AMERICA

When you are young and strong and fit and you feel sick you don't feel the need to go to the doctor. You treat yourself, thinking that because you are young, and strong and fit you will be OK.

When you are old and feel sick, you stay away from the doctor because you are afraid the doctor is going to give you some really bad news. So you stay away until it's too late! Especially if you're afraid the doctor is going to tell you it's stage four cancer, or irreparable damage to the arteries, or if you've been on a drinking binge for forty years the doctor is probably going to tell you that it's too late to save your liver. He could have saved you if you had come to see him twenty years ago!

Think of America today as your body and Dinesh D'Sousa as your doctor who has some very, very bad news: you're deathly ill! Listen to him. Read this book. Find out what is causing you to be sick, and what it is going to take to get well.

Learn everything you can about your disease and how to defeat it or else you are going to get sicker until nobody is going to be able to treat you.

It's not too late yet, but you are going to have to be "all in." You need to be well informed about the disease, its causes and symptoms, and totally committed to the treatment D'Souza is laying out for you or else you are going to die.

According to D'Sousa, the disease that's killing America is socialism. It's not just any old socialism, but an especially virulent and deadly strain called "Identity Socialism." Like all socialisms, the ideas are borrowed from Karl Marx and others that go back even earlier.

Unlike other socialisms, Identity Socialism doesn't claim that the working class is the victim of exploitation. They know that the working class today is too well off to buy into their insane nostrums.

Working class Americans today are more likely to vote Republican than to fall for the same dishonest claims of the socialists currently controlling the Democrat Party.

The socialists have written off—and smeared—the white working class as racist and bigoted.

This review of *The United States of Socialism* will empower you to be "all in" in the fight against the forces that want to turn America into a socialist nightmare.

IDENTITY POLITICS AND SOCIALISM

D'Souza exposes the strategy and methods Identity Socialists are using to take over America: they have invented a whole new set of victims. They are victims of Christian morality and free market capitalism. The Identity Socialists claim that every minority group in society is a victim.

They isolate the victimology of each group: racial minorities, sexual deviants, the psychologically damaged, the Bohemians and the Avant-garde, feminists, teachers and professors, government bureaucrats, artists, celebrities, writers and journalists, media personalities, illegal immigrants.

Then the Identity Socialists convince them that they can only become happy if they overthrow any vestige of Christian and traditional morality, destroy the culture, and with it the system of free enterprise capitalism that made America great.

Dinesh D'Souza has brilliantly observed and analyzed the real reasons why Identity Socialism poses such a threat to the American way of life: "it cuts across economic and cultural divisions and is more revolutionary than simply taking over the means of production."

D'Souza reminds us that Socialism, unlike other political or economic systems, has been utterly discredited; and unlike other systems, including feudalism and slavery, it was discredited in a much shorter period.

"No serious person today would advocate the return of slavery," says D'Souza. "No serious person would say the problem with slavery is that it was poorly implemented! Next time we will get it right! But that's how its advocates package socialism: the newest form of slavery."

D'Souza claims there have been 25 national experiments with Socialism, all ending in unmitigated disaster. In case you think he is just making this up, this is a heavily footnoted book. He documents all of his claims.

Socialism is inherently totalitarian but also murderous. The Soviets killed at least 20 million of their own citizens. Mao killed over 80 million. The National Socialists (the Nazis) killed a similar number. Socialism not only makes people miserable, it also kills a lot of people.

For the starkest example of the chasm between socialism and freedom we only have to look at North and South Korea. D'Sousa claims that South Korea is 20 times richer than North Korea. I think he's being generous. It's probably more like a hundred times richer.

When a border guard recently defected to South Korea, he was discovered to be malnourished and full of worms. And he was presumably a member of one of their best military outfits!

South Koreans are obviously much freer. They are also healthier, taller, more physically fit and live about 12 years longer. Nobody, absolutely nobody risks their lives to escape South Korea to head north to North Korea.

Despite the failed history of socialism, at no time in our history has socialism been more popular. Polling indicates that 43% of the American people have a positive attitude toward socialism.

That's because the left controls our educational institutions, our media and entertainment industry, many large corporations, and has even made serious inroads within our churches. They have been able to re-package socialism in terms of identity politics, dividing America so that it becomes easier to conquer.

This divide and conquer strategy is being fought in the name of "Identity Socialism." Take note of how American Socialists—especially key people with major access to the mainstream media—are packaging their poison to make it appealing to the average American.

The latest socialist theory, according to D'Souza? "They call it 'the end of work.'" Automation will take over every job, including the service sector. The only 'work' people will engage in will be as consumers, living off the productive labor of robots.

Congresswoman Alexandra Ocasio-Cortes tells the American worker, in exchange for such future 'work,' "people will be entitled to receive everything they need for free."

The mass abundance created by automation will make this possible, assures this pied piper of Socialism and key leader of today's Democratic Party. Innovative capitalism will make socialism not only possible but necessary. Or so they tell us.

The founder of the socialist magazine *Jacobin* says "socialism is an ideology of radical democracy." It's "about the democratic control of every single facet of our life," according to Ugo Okere who ran the Chicago City Council in 2019. "Small wonder that our Founding Fathers feared the tyranny of the majority more than the tyranny of kings," says D'Souza.

The Founders of our nation never recognize there is some "will of the people" that can directly govern society. And if there were, they would never agree to a right of the majority to gang up on the minority and steal their property.

That's the whole point of their ingenious "checks and balances," the supposedly unfair U.S. Senate (where each state, regardless of population, has two U.S. Senators) and the very misunderstood Electoral College. The founders did not create a Democracy without limits, but a Republic with constraints on the power of government and the power of the majority.

For Madison, democracy is mob rule, "incompatible with personal security or the rights of property...."

The first object of government, according to James Madison, is "the protection of different and unequal faculties of acquiring property." Alexander Hamilton wrote, "a prosperous commerce was a primary object of the political concerns of statesmen." Even Jefferson, a fan of the French Revolution, opposed any government schemes to redistribute income.

WHAT IS IDENTITY SOCIALISM?

This section will be short and simple: The Identity Socialists exploit diversity in order to eliminate diversity, eliminate the human personality, and absorb everyone into an amorphous mass, except for them. They will be rich and in charge and free to do whatever they want with us.

In summary, as D'Souza's book details, the socialist left is excluding their opponents from debate, enforcing a foreign and alien ideology on the American people, and making them look and feel like foreigners in their own country.

PROPERTY RIGHTS ARE PEOPLE RIGHTS

The Founders were primarily concerned with "the cultivation of the human personality, and the idea that property rights are no less fundamental than civil rights and civil liberties. It makes no sense to say I own my own religious and political opinions but don't own my labor and have a right to the fruits of it," writes D'Souza.

In short, the Founding of our nation is "a nightmare for the Socialists," according to the author. But since socialists everywhere are liars, thugs, gangsters and thieves, they tend to get their way by using propaganda appealing to man's baser instincts. They also like to get very rich themselves.

American socialists don't point to the Nordic countries for the ideal socialist societies. They used to love the Soviet Union and Communist China. Now they absolutely love Venezuela.

Venezuela has precisely the kind of division socialism that American socialists want. Bill Ayers, former violent member of the Weather Underground, one of the most powerful and influential people in America when it comes to setting education policy and standards, the one who jump-started Obama's political career, "had numerous conversations with senior education officials under Venezuela's late dictator, Hugo Chavez.

"Ayers could not have been more excited about the socialist indoctrination in Venezuelan schools," D'Souza says.

Jimmy Carter visited Venezuela and endorsed the fraudulent election results of 2012.

D'Souza's wife hails from Venezuela. He knows from family experience just how bad things are there, and why. "Hugo Chavez turned Venezuela into a racially polarized society. He vilified whites. He demonized the productive class, mostly Europeans, Americans and Venezuelans in the oil industry. Chavez then took over the oil industry and re-wrote their contracts. Some big companies moved their operations out of Venezuela."

"Chavez got rid of the trained and experienced managers and put his political cronies in charge, who then ran the oil companies into the ground. Then he began to confiscate land and property," says D'Souza.

It's futile to oppose this, like the science-fiction Borg of Star Trek fame ("resistance is futile").

"Inexorably, Chavez packed the Supreme Court and re-wrote the constitution to eliminate civil liberties in Venezuela. He confiscated guns. If you blamed the government for shortages, he sent armed thugs, mostly criminals called the *collectivos*, to terrorize you."

D'Souza knows this first hand. Some of his Venezuelan relatives have joined the Chavistas. Others have been victimized by them.

In Venezuela, as in America, "public servants" become rich. The top ones in the Venezuelan government live at the scale of the richest people in the world.

The late Hugo Chavez's family owns 17 country estates, totaling more than 100,000 acres. Forbes named Chavez one of the 400 richest people in the world. He looted $2 billion from the Venezuelan people. In Venezuela, the top 1% are all socialists.

Unlike the American founders, the socialists say property rights are the enemy of the people. America's heritage teaches property rights—the fruit of the labor of the person—are "people" rights.

AREN'T SOCIALISTS THE MODERN-DAY ROBBER BARONS?

Socialists aren't dumb. They know that most Americans would not want to go to their neighbor's house and steal food from his refrigerator and burglarize whatever they want. It's wrong. So they create a story line that those who have more than you have somehow stolen that from you and from all of society. Not to mention you are an evil, wicked Nazi and a bigot. Now it is OK to rob you, which is basically, what Socialism proposes. This reports D'Souza, is a combination of "envy and entitlement… their peculiar talent."

D'Souza brilliantly exposes how the socialist left labels American entrepreneurs as being greedy and selfish—precisely what they are themselves. And they seek to license all Americans to join them in looting those who have accumulated any savings, whether it is equity in your house, your retirement plan, your medical account, even debasing Medicare by "spreading around the wealth" for "Medicare for all."

A Review of the Book *United States of Socialism*

VICTIMS IN NEED OF RESCUE

The new American socialists have no choice but to tear America down, says D'Souza, because they want to replace it with something totally foreign to our Founding Fathers' vision. That's why New York governor Mario Cuomo said "We're not going to make America great again, it was never that great." They teach a different, ominous, Twilight Zone form of American history that bears very slight resemblance to reality.

D'Souza is correct in revealing that the Socialists' version of U.S. history is one of oppression of victims. The Indians. The New York Irish during the Civil War. The slaves they claim were ignored in the Declaration of Independence and the original Constitution. Deserting servicemen during the U.S.-Mexico war. Women and children being "forced" to work during the Industrial revolution. The devastation of two World Wars and later the oppression of Latin America by—you guessed it—the United States of America. And of course, the immigrants, legal and illegal (which they call "migrants" and "undocumented workers" even though over 50% of the latter are on some form of welfare).

The Socialist version of history, being taught to our children today, to new arrivals in America, to inner city blacks and to all Americans, is dismal, bleak, dark, foreboding. Everything is the fault of America, our most successful entrepreneurs, and those leaders that an earlier generation revered and admired. With these teachings, no wonder so many young people have been rioting, defacing, and destroying statues and monuments all over the country.

The twin message of the socialist left is to hate America and tear everything down, and put them in power. Dinesh D'Souza's book is a terrific attempt to show them how wrong these teachings are.

LINCOLN AND DOUGLASS

It is no accident or mistake by crazed mobs that statues of President Abraham Lincoln, Union General and later President U.S. Grant and even black slave-runaway and self-made man Frederick Douglass, are among those defaced and torn down by the so-called protestors of the socialist left.

Lincoln of course, is the first Republican President, who freed the slaves. Grant is the Union General he appointed, who finally started winning battles and helped Lincoln win the war and free the slaves. And the man who today should be the most famous of the former slaves, Frederick Douglass, became an admirer of Lincoln and fiercely pro-American. He became an advocate for black success without government programs and an advocate for the Republican Party of Abraham Lincoln.

They tear these statues down and attack these American heroes because they cannot debate them. It is the liberal-Democrats of their day who defended slavery and opposed equality for blacks. It is American heroes Lincoln, Grant and Douglass, who were the role models of that day—and should be today as well—for an America open to advancement for all colors, races and creeds. They can't handle the truth so they smear our American heroes. Once again, D'Souza explains the reality of American history splendidly.

They especially hate Frederick Douglass, who asked just after the end of the Civil War, "What should be done with the slaves"? His answer does not endear him to today's socialist left: "Do nothing with us! Your doing with us has already played mischief with us. Do nothing with us… if the Negro cannot stand on his own legs, let him fall. All I ask is, give him a chance to stand on his own legs."

SOCIALISTS WANT TO STEAL ALL OF YOUR MONEY FOR THEMSELVES

American Socialists like getting rich. Michael Moore made over $50 million making documentaries that bash capitalism. Bernie Sanders and his wife are multi-millionaires and own three homes, including a lakefront summer pad. Elizabeth Warren has accumulated $12 million bashing free markets and passing herself off as a Native American.

The Clintons have made money every which way, by selling pardons, by siphoning off charitable donations intended for poor Haitians, exorbitant fees from Moscow allies while his wife was U.S. Secretary of State and so on. The Clintons have made over $200 million since leaving office.

The Obamas own a $2.5 million Chicago home, a D.C. home worth $8 million, and a $12 million beachfront property on Martha's Vineyard. They are addicted to luxury vacations.

"Middle Class" Joe Biden owns a 12,000 square foot home in McLean, Virginia with a gym and sauna and parking for 20 cars. He owns a beach house in Delaware to complement his 7,000 square foot lakeside home.

His sons have become multi-millionaires by trading on Biden's political name and connections, making money from the governments of Ukraine and Communist China, among others.

Socialism is good business!

D'Souza reports the unvarnished truth in the *United States of Socialism*: it's the socialists who are the greedy, selfish, hypocritical bastards, not the "capitalists." They are parasites, feeding off the wealth of society while reviling the free market system that made it all possible.

Obama claimed by electing him as President the sea levels would begin to subside. He tried to scare us with the threat of all of our coastal cities being inundated as a result of something they used to call "global warming."

Only Obama doesn't believe in it himself. As D'Souza asks, why else would he invest $12 million in an ocean front compound on Martha's Vineyard?

Such rank hypocrisy is typical of socialists. Only you and I have to pay through the nose so they can indulge their hypocritical greed.

Barack Obama was deified by the media and the Democrat Party. The Nobel Committee even awarded him the Peace Prize shortly after he was sworn in.

Why? He accomplished nothing as President. Ah—for being Obama he was virtually deified, glorified, worshiped! Then he proceeded to bomb Libya and Syria.

Socialism is always for you and me, not for them. Where did this come from? It comes from Americans who lived lives of privilege and hated the Founding principles of our nation, beginning with Woodrow Wilson.

Woodrow Wilson, we learn in this book, was the first president to attack the founding principles of our nation: "We are not bound to adhere to the doctrines held by the signers of the Declaration of Independence." Wilson believed society should be run by enlightened planners, not by laws, or the principles in the Constitution.

So-called "progressive" government under Wilson instituted the Federal Reserve Bank to regulate money away from the sight or say of elected officials accountable to anyone. It instituted the "progressive" income tax. It created the Federal Trade Commission to oversee industry, all of which led to the fourth branch of government, what has become the "Deep State."

Wilson also introduced racial segregation to the federal government, including the military branches. This combination of white nationalism and progressivism came to dominate the Democrat Party.

Wilson introduced creeping socialism. FDR called the socialist agenda "a Second Bill of Rights." Everything on Bernie Sanders' list is from FDR's "Second Bill of Rights."

Under Roosevelt, reports D'Souza, the government would take care of everyone's needs, giving them "freedom from fear." The primary vehicle was the Social Security system, which was promised as a personal retirement account, but was not set up that way—intentionally. Roosevelt raised the top income tax rate to 80%! He wanted all income at the highest level to be taxed at 99.5%!

The purpose of confiscatory taxation was to create loyal voters—the recipients of government generosity—for the Democrat Party. The simple socialist idea was to take money away from those who had it, and give it to his own constituency who would then reward Roosevelt and his Democrat Party with their loyalty and their votes.

"FDR also leaned heavily on white identity politics. Blacks were excluded from New Deal programs. Social Security did not pay benefits to domestic workers and farm workers, most of whom were black. Republicans repealed those provisions in 1954." D'Souza reminds us that it's the Democrats who have always treated blacks as inferior and the Republicans who have consistently stood for civil rights.

Every Democrat Senator from the South voted against the Civil Rights Act. The only reason it passed is because the Republican Senate Minority Leader, Everett Dirkson, supported it and got the necessary Republican votes.

Demolishing the myth of the Democratic Party as friends to blacks, D'Souza reports Roosevelt appointed a member of the KKK to the Supreme Court. Roosevelt told Hugo Black some of his best friends and supporters were strong members of the KKK.

It is now fashionable for American socialists to excoriate fascism, but the *United States of*

Socialism lays out the truth—the enthusiasm of FDR and New Deal progressives for Mussolini's fascism. "FDR and Mussolini formed a mutual admiration society," D'Souza writes, "reviewing each other's books and praising each other as ideological soul mates."

Because fascism has become toxic, FDR's biographers say little or nothing about his accurate view of fascism as "somewhat parallel to the Communist experiment in Russia."

SOCIALIST PRESIDENT WILSON VS ENTREPRENEUR FORD

One of the items missing from Wilson's biography is he opposed the development of the automobile. To him it was the "picture of arrogance and wealth." Wilson claimed to be a man of the people. "He thought he knew what they wanted and what they ought to want and he saw no reason why the masses would ever want, or ever be able to afford an automobile," says D'Souza.

"Entrepreneur Ford's genius was to create a demand for an affordable automobile that at the time, nobody wanted. By 1916, Ford's Model T was selling for less than $400. The car has probably been the most democratizing force in history, not the Democrat Party, and certainly not socialism."

Punchy D'Souza bluntly warns: "Identity Socialism demonizes the working class. The typical socialist today is not a union guy who wants higher wages but a transsexual ecofeminist who marches in Antifa and Black Lives Matter marches and throws bricks" at his/its/her political opponents.

Elizabeth Warren tweeted "Black trans and cis women, gender non-conforming, and nonbinary people are the backbone of our democracy."

Michael Moore says working class Americans are not coming back to the Democrat Party. Moore defines the Democrat base as women, young people and people of color.

HERBERT MARCUSE: FATHER OF IDENTITY SOCIALISM

Identity Socialists want to invert the former hierarchy. Whiteness, maleness and heterosexuality are now viewed as pathological, as forms of oppression. The great shift occurred in the 1960's. One man influenced this shift more than any other: Herbert Marcuse.

Considered the father of the emergent "New Left" that came to dominate today's Democratic Party, Dr. Herbert Marcuse influenced a whole generation of young communists in America: Bill Ayers, Abbie Hoffman, Tom Hayden, Angela Davis and others.

Interestingly, it was Ronald Reagan—then Governor of California—who got Marcuse fired from his position at UC Berkeley. Marcuse retained his celebrity status and influence. His socialism is the socialism we have here in America now, which dominates one of the two major political parties in America.

Communist founding theoretician Karl Marx predicted a full-blown worker revolt. It never happened. Later, Lenin recognized it would never happen, that workers would never achieve "revolutionary consciousness."

A professional class of activists and fighters would have to do it for them, serving as a revolutionary vanguard. This was a radical break from Marx's theory of the inevitability of the revolution.

The Italian Communist Antonio Gramsci claimed capitalists did not rule society solely on the basis of economic power, but also through "bourgeois values." Although Marx had said much the same thing in The Communist Manifesto it took figures like Gramsci and Marcuse to popularize the theme of cultural revolution as a prerequisite for establishing a communist society. Economics, Gramsci said, is a subset of culture.

Same sex marriage, childhood sex changes, gay pride parades, these are all necessary components of the Identity Socialist agenda. Destroy the culture first, then you can take over the economy.

Marcuse psychologized Karl Marx, says D'Souza. He understood that once people stopped believing in God they lived in a constant state of uncertainty and high anxiety. "He targeted the "Bohemian" type, the avant-garde, the artists and intellectuals who hated industrial civilization and considered themselves superior to businessmen and shopkeepers."

"Bohemia," wrote Henri Murger, "leads either to Academia, the Hospital or the Morgue." Marcuse understood Bohemia as a cultural ideal, and offered a refuge to psychological casualties too disturbed to undertake productive employment or conform to the moral rules of society. Marcuse called it "The Great Refusal—the visceral repudiation of the free market society."

At the time, there were scarcely enough Bohemians to hold a demonstration, let alone make a revolution.

Marcuse turned to the young political and pop idols of the 60's, along with college students in general, to serve as the shock troops of his cultural revolution. "They already lived in socialist communes—called universities—and took their amenities for granted. They were alienated and seeking fulfillment," says D'Souza.

If you wonder why your son or daughter turned left in college, ask no more. That's what happens when you live in a quasi-Soviet commune for four years where traditional American values are constantly ridiculed and attacked.

Marcuse portrayed Ho Chi Minh and the Vietcong as heroes, fighting against American hegemony. Totally perverting the word, they were the true "freedom" fighters.

With Bohemians and college students on his side, who else? He targeted the Black Power movement, feminists, and environmentalists as part of his vanguard of the revolution.

By inverting Freud, Marcuse is actually behind all of the bizarre political manifestations of sexuality: group sex, pansexuality, polymorphous sexuality, all of which Freud called perversions.

Today, Marcuse's socialist dream has been realized in a way that Marx, Eugene Debs, FDR, and Henry Wallace could not have imagined. "Marcuse was always, first and foremost, a conventional socialist who believed only in the collective. But it was his genius to create identity politics as the vehicle."

SOCIALISM AND THE GREEN NEW DEAL

The Green New Deal is the most expansive socialist agenda since the Nazi 25-point platform of 1920. The price tag of $90 trillion for the first ten-year period is irrelevant. We cannot afford not to do it, they insist! The planet will die otherwise.

D'Souza goes on to report The Green New Deal advocates claim their program to be "scientific," just as Marx claimed 150 years ago. Marx claimed his "scientific" system was beyond criticism. Green New Dealers call skeptics "science deniers."

Fortunately, scientific and common-sense observation demonstrates the fear mongering by the environmentalists about the threat of global warming is proven to be just that. Examples: there are four times as many polar bears now as there were in 1960; the Obamas just paid $12 million for a coastal mansion; marginally higher CO_2 levels have led to the greening of the earth and a shrinking of the Sahara Desert.

Yet socialists offer only two options: extinction or socialism: you get to choose!

SOCIALISTS AND ILLEGAL IMMIGRATION

Illegal immigration also animates identity socialists. Marcuse never foresaw this opportunity. But he would have jumped on it in a minute. Even Obama enforced immigration law to some extent.

"Today's Democrats want an entirely open border," says D'Souza, "partly out of self-interest: it means a permanent Democrat political majority once illegals are given citizenship; it also conforms to their ideological beliefs."

"Socialists and labor unions have traditionally opposed illegal immigration because it hurts their working-class supporters. Marx would have been outraged. This allows native workers to blame foreigners, not the capitalist system, for their misery."

"The Identity Socialists hate Trump's wall. Not because they think walls don't work, but because they know they do. Society builds walls all the time. They just aren't so obvious."

"Try to get into Harvard or Stanford and you will discover there is a wall higher than Trump could ever build! Nobody ever snuck into Stanford, went to classes for four years, and graduated."

Democrats know they cannot change immigration laws through normal political channels. They openly defy existing laws. They portray enforcement of immigration laws as hateful, racist and Nazi-like.

D'Souza convincingly states the obvious: "An illegal immigrant is no more an undocumented worker than someone who breaks into my house is an undocumented owner."

A Review of the Book *United States of Socialism*

But the Identity Socialists believe illegals have a right to migrate to rich countries as a form of "reparations" to compensate them for American imperialism and hegemony.

But Mexicans who ended up in America after the Mexican War were immeasurably better off.

A critical part of creating a ruling majority is to create new classes of racial and especially sexual victims. They want to replace your moral code with theirs. Typical is their argument that men who call themselves women should compete with women in sports. If you oppose it, they attack you, threaten you and destroy your life.

BE HOPEFUL

D'Souza says that we have yet to develop stage four cancer.

Socialists argue, as did Marx, that a socialist future is inevitable. But it isn't. A thief wearing a mask can get away with it for a while. Unmasked, he cannot.

The *United States of Socialism* unmasks the socialists.

WHAT CAN YOU DO?

We cannot be silent when someone says socialism is a more moral system than free markets, capitalism and entrepreneurship. It isn't. Dinesh D'Souza provides the proof in this book.

Know the socialists' true goals and don't be afraid to tell people. Their goal is to turn foreigners into natives and natives into foreigners. By creating a new sense of belonging to an identity group, the sane ones among us become alienated from our own society.

FDR preached exactly the same virulent ideology. He told Americans who opposed his New Deal socialism to emigrate. Good riddance! He actually said this!

Socialists praise virtually anything and everything that is illegal, except not paying your taxes, of course. And if you or I object? The plan is to put you and me into re-education camps. That's not extremism talking. That's history.

It's not Nordic Socialism we are talking about here. Bernie Sanders didn't honeymoon in Sweden, he honeymooned in the Soviet Union! The current mayor of New York City honeymooned in Cuba!

What is the socialist temptation? It's to "annihilate one's conscience by feeling justified in living off other people's work." That's because socialists are very good at producing words, but utterly useless in producing wealth.

And what do their words produce: envy and a sense of entitlement. They won't admit this because if they did, they would have to admit that the greed and selfishness they apply to entrepreneurs more accurately describes themselves.

AFTERWORD: A CALL TO ACTION

by Hon. Gary Giordano

Former State Representatives (AZ)
Executive Director, White House Watch Fund

We have to use every social media vehicle at our disposal to bring the truth to light. If you have 50 friends on Facebook, or 500 contacts on LinkedIn, then reach out to them. Make sure they have a copy of this pocketbook. They can carry the message to their friends and contacts.

Don't let the socialists in the media, or in your neighborhood, or in your own family intimidate you.

Join groups that magnify your influence. It doesn't cost much. You can begin by ordering more copies of this pocketbook and distribute it to your friends. You can make a donation so millions of freedom-loving Americans can read this handy paperback to become informed and motivated.

Support petition drives. They work! Call your Congressman and Senators and demand they oppose President Biden's socialist proposals. Don't for a minute assume it's enough to privately cast your vote and then go home, thinking that the politicians alone will save America.

Every time you get a petition in the mail that you agree with, why not go an extra step beyond just signing and returning it in the inevitable, self-addressed envelope they provided you? Why not use that information to write a letter to the editor, a post on Facebook, a short message to your elected officials?

Get more involved in your Church and voluntary organizations. Socialists have been actively taking over boards that control our churches and civic organizations for decades. The more people you make friends with the more people you can influence.

D'Souza wants to go after the Deep State criminals who have tried to terrorize and obstruct former President Trump, and many of his staff and key advisors. And his book shows you the motivation and purpose of those who would replace the Trump policies with new Biden socialism.

Get a copy of this book, *The United States of Socialism*. Get several copies and give them out as gifts.

Have faith and confidence and hope. Be strong in the knowledge America is the greatest nation on earth. It has provided the greatest amount of freedom and prosperity in the history of the planet.

What is at stake right now is whether America will become socialist or whether these proposals can be blocked and whether Americans will reject those who propose socialism in the 2022 and 2024 elections.

Just as our men and women in uniform have made tremendous sacrifices to win freedom and to defend it, now is the time for you to enlist. This is war. It's time to put on your fatigues and go to battle. The *United States of Socialism* by Dinesh D'Souza, is a clarion call to action.

A ringing defense of freedom and the truth about the Joe Biden socialists who hate it

New Biden Era Edition

A Review of the Book

UNITED STATES OF SOCIALISM

Who's Behind It. Why It's Evil. How to Stop It.

by Dinesh D'Souza

Book Review by **WILLIAM E. SARACINO**
Executive Vice President, White House Watch Fund

Introduction by **SANT GUPTA**
(past) Master of Ceremonies, Freedom Leadership Conference

Another pocketbook by White House Watch Fund:

A Review of the Book, the United States of Socialism
Who's Behind it. Why It's Evil. How to Stop it. by Dinesh D'Souza

Book Review by William E. Saracino, Executive Vice President, White House Watch Fund.

Donation $5 for one. 3 for $10. 10 for $20. 100 for $150.
Plus Postage and handling of $3 plus 10%.
Send your donation check and request to:

White House Watch Fund
Freedom Center, Fulfilment Dept.
P.O. Box 820
Stuarts Draft, VA 24477-0820

Another pocketbook by White House Watch Fund:

Big Lies
How Trump Overcame Liberal Lies to Fight the China Virus (Covid-19)

Donation $5 for one. 3 for $10. 10 for $20. 100 for $150.
Plus Postage and handling of $3 plus 10%.
Send your donation check and request to:

White House Watch Fund
Freedom Center, Fulfilment Dept.
P.O. Box 820
Stuarts Draft, VA 24477-0820